Franklin D. Roosevelt

Our PRESIDENTS

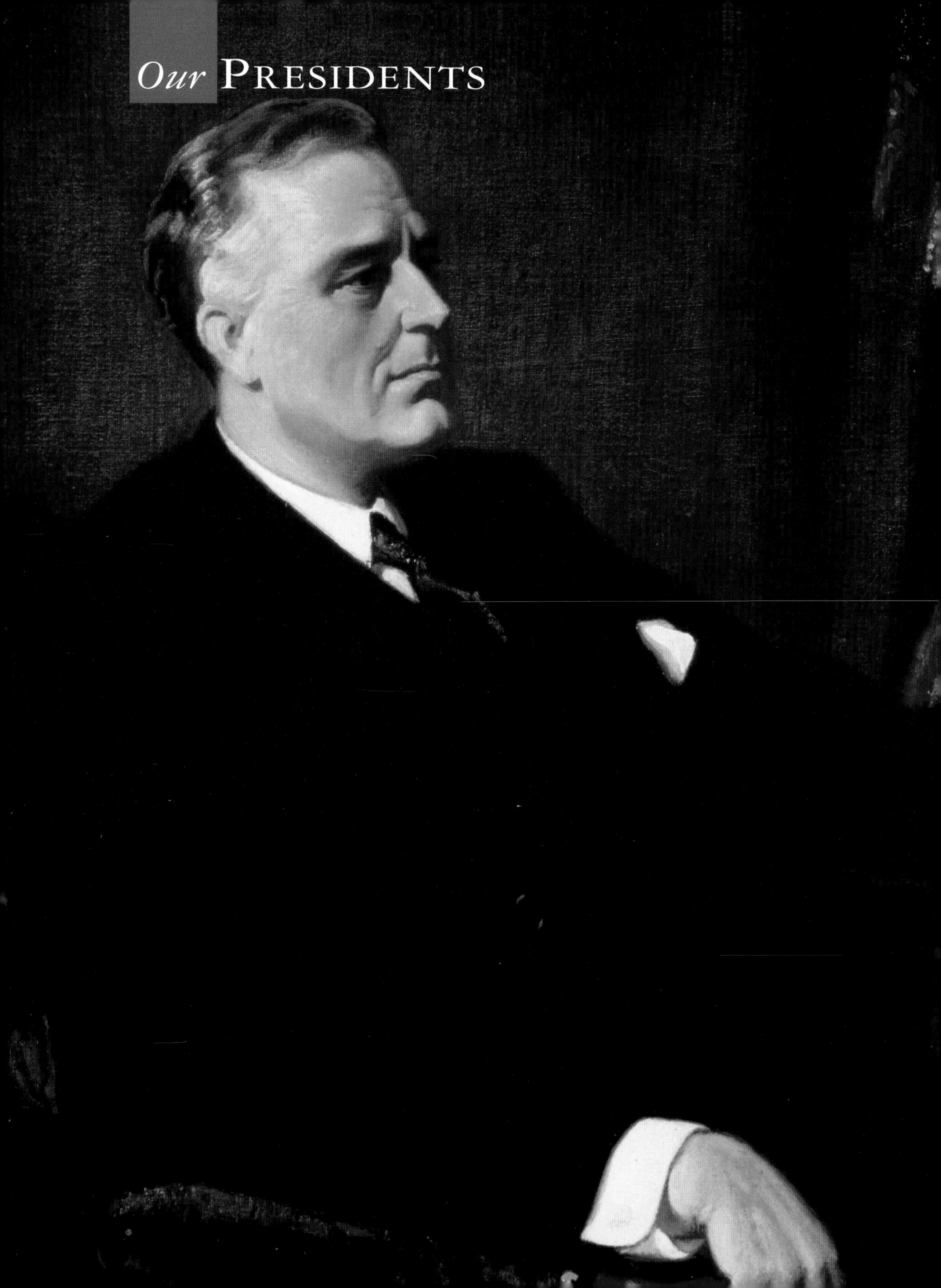

FRANKLIN D. *Roosevelt*

OUR THIRTY-SECOND PRESIDENT

By Melissa Maupin

SPIRIT
of America™

The Child's World®, Inc.
Chanhassen, Minnesota

6

FRANKLIN D. *Roosevelt*

Published in the United States of America by The Child's World®, Inc.
PO Box 326 • Chanhassen, MN 55317-0326 • 800-599-READ • www.childsworld.com

Acknowledgments
The Creative Spark: Mary Francis-DeMarois, Project Director; Elizabeth Sirimarco Budd, Series Editor; Robert Court, Design and Art Direction; Janine Graham, Page Layout; Jennifer Moyers, Production

The Child's World®, Inc.: Mary Berendes, Publishing Director; Red Line Editorial, Fact Research; Cindy Klingel, Curriculum Advisor; Robert Noyed, Historical Advisor

Photos
Cover: White House Collection, courtesy White House Historical Association; Bettmann/Corbis: 35; Corbis: 37; Courtesy of Franklin D. Roosevelt Library and Museum: 6, 7, 9, 11, 12, 13, 15, 18, 19, 20, 21, 23, 24, 29, 31, 32, 33, 34, 36; Library of Congress: 27; © Oscar White/CORBIS: 28

Registration
The Child's World®, Inc., Spirit of America™, and their associated logos are the sole property and registered trademarks of The Child's World®, Inc.

Library of Congress Cataloging-in-Publication Data
Maupin, Melissa, 1958–
    Franklin D. Roosevelt : our thirty-second president / by Melissa Maupin.
        p. cm.
    Includes bibliographical references and index.
    ISBN 1-56766-866-6 (alk. paper)
    1. Roosevelt, Franklin D. (Franklin Delano), 1882–1945—Juvenile literature. 2. Presidents—United States—Biography—Juvenile literature. [1. Roosevelt, Franklin D. (Franklin Delano), 1882–1945.
2. Presidents.] I. Title.
    E807 .M34 2001
    973.917'092–dc21

                                        00-010947

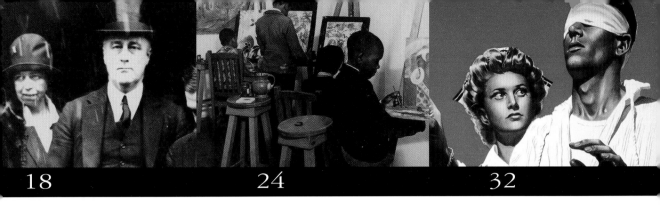

18   24   32

Contents

Chapter ONE

Wealthy Roots

Young Franklin was the only child of James and Sara Roosevelt. He admired his father and felt very close to his mother. "I received a love and companionship that was rare between parent and child," he later remembered.

FRANKLIN DELANO ROOSEVELT WAS ELECTED president of the United States during one of the saddest and most difficult times in history —the Great **Depression.** During the Depression, millions of Americans lost their jobs. Many went homeless and hungry. As president, Roosevelt felt the pain and suffering of the American people. He did everything in his power to help the country recover from the Depression. "The test of our progress is not whether we add more abundance of those who have much," he said, "it is whether we provide enough for those who have too little."

Although Roosevelt was dedicated to helping poor Americans, he had never been poor himself. In fact, Roosevelt grew up in a wealthy family. His father, James, was the

successful president of a railroad company. He had enough money to supply young Franklin with anything he wanted or needed.

Franklin Roosevelt was born in 1882 in Hyde Park, New York. He was schooled at his country mansion, as was the custom in wealthy families at the time. His mother, Sara, taught him when he was young. As he grew older, nannies and tutors took over the job of educating him. When he finished his studies, Franklin enjoyed collecting stamps and scouring the local woods in search of wildlife. Each summer, he could hardly wait to start the family vacation. The Roosevelts

As a young boy, Franklin had every advantage. He spent his first 14 years under the watchful eye of his parents. He did not even attend school, but took his lessons at home. The Roosevelts are shown here at their home in Hyde Park.

7

▸ Franklin's mother, Sara Delano, was 26 years younger than her husband James. He was a widower with one son, Franklin's half-brother James.

▸ Roosevelt was a big, 10-pound baby. His birth was very difficult for him and for his mother. He was born with a bluish color, and the doctor feared he might not be alive. He blew into Franklin's lungs, and Franklin finally gave a healthy cry. The delivery was so difficult that Sara had no more children after Franklin.

traveled to Campobello, their summer home on the Canadian coast. There Franklin learned to sail and dreamed of becoming a real sailor one day.

When Franklin was 12, James Roosevelt wanted to send him to boarding school, but Sara refused. She couldn't bear to be without her son. Finally, at age 14, the Roosevelts enrolled Franklin in the Groton School. He was older than most of the boys in his classes and had a difficult time making friends. He did meet a boy named Lothrop Brown at Groton. Lothrop and Franklin became best friends and remained close throughout Roosevelt's life.

After graduation, Franklin attended Harvard College. He shared his large, elegant apartment with Lothrop Brown. Roosevelt made only average grades. He spent more energy on his social life than on his studies. He also worked hard to win a position as a reporter for the school newspaper, the *Crimson.*

Near the end of his first term at Harvard, Franklin received tragic news. His father had suffered a severe heart attack. Franklin finished the semester and then rushed home to be with his family. One month later, James

Roosevelt died with Sara and Franklin at his bedside. The Christmas holidays proved to be a sad time for Franklin and his mother. Without James, Sara was alone. To be near her son, she moved to Cambridge, Massachusetts. For the rest of her life, Sara lived with or very close to Franklin.

At Harvard, Franklin dreamed of being a member of the social club, the Porcellian. Roosevelt's father and his cousin, Theodore Roosevelt, had both been members. Many students dreamed of being members of the Porcellian, but few were asked to join. The members eagerly asked Lothrop Brown to join, but they did not ask Franklin. Naturally, Franklin was upset. As at Groton, he could not understand why the other students rejected him.

During his Harvard years, Roosevelt fell in love with his future wife, Eleanor Roosevelt. Eleanor was his fifth cousin. As children, they had played together at family gatherings. Roosevelt hadn't seen Eleanor in several years. On a train trip from Washington to New York, he grew bored

Like Franklin, Eleanor Roosevelt was from a wealthy New York family, but her childhood was a difficult one. By the time she was 10 years old, Eleanor had lost both her parents. She and her two brothers went to live with their grandmother.

▶ At Groton, Franklin Roosevelt already had a strong interest in **politics.** One reason for his keen interest was his cousin Theodore (Teddy) Roosevelt. Teddy had long been active in politics, and he became a hero during the Spanish-American War in 1898. In this war, America helped Cuba fight for its freedom from Spain. Teddy Roosevelt led a troop of soldiers called "The Rough Riders" in a victorious battle in Cuba. Later he was elected vice president. He became president after William McKinley was killed in 1901.

▶ Franklin Roosevelt graduated from Harvard in just three years. Most college students take four years to finish their studies.

and decided to explore the train. In one car, he was surprised to discover the grown-up Eleanor sitting by herself. He sat with her, and they visited for the rest of the trip. After their travels, they continued to date. Roosevelt took Eleanor to dances and parties. Eleanor may have seemed an odd match for Franklin. Franklin was a dashing young man. He was tall, handsome, and very social. He chatted easily with others and enjoyed attending parties and entertaining friends. Eleanor, on the other hand, was considered plain looking. She hated her chin, which she called weak, and the way her upper teeth stuck out. Eleanor was also quiet and shy. She felt uncomfortable at social events.

When Franklin proposed to Eleanor, his mother was upset. She did not think Eleanor was the right match for her only son. She tried to get Franklin to date other young ladies, but he refused. Franklin and Eleanor were married on St. Patrick's Day, March 17, 1905. They went on a tour of Europe for their honeymoon.

After graduating from Harvard, Franklin attended Columbia Law School. In 1907, he passed the state law exam and left before graduation to practice law. He became a law clerk at Carter, Ledyard, and Milburn, a New York firm. Meanwhile, Franklin and Eleanor had settled into married life. Eleanor had their first child, Anna, in 1906. Over the following nine years, the Roosevelts had five more children: James, Franklin Jr. (who died as an infant), Elliott, a second Franklin Jr., and John.

Eleanor and Franklin worked to build a happy marriage, but Sara Roosevelt did not make their job easy. She was very close to Franklin and had strong opinions about how he and Eleanor should live. She made household decisions without asking Eleanor's opinion. She also tried to take over the raising of Eleanor and Franklin's children. Sometimes Eleanor fought back, but Franklin rarely supported her. Eleanor often felt alone and frustrated.

Although Sara Roosevelt did not think Eleanor and Franklin were a good match, they married on March 17, 1905. The photo above was taken during their honeymoon to Europe.

11

Chapter TWO

Politics and War

Franklin Roosevelt entered politics in 1910, when he was elected a New York State senator.

FRANKLIN ROOSEVELT QUICKLY GREW TIRED OF working in the law firm. He craved the excitement of politics. He quit the firm and ran for the New York State Senate. He **campaigned** across the state with this promise: "I am pledged to no man, no special interest, and to no boss." At that time, powerful men called "bosses" made the political decisions in their cities. Roosevelt pledged to think for himself and not to be the puppet of political bosses. His campaign worked. He won the election and began work as a state senator.

While campaigning for his second **term** in 1911, Roosevelt and Eleanor caught typhoid fever, a serious illness. He was forced to stay in bed for several weeks instead of campaigning. He called a newspaperman

12

As Franklin's career in politics took off, his family was growing. Eleanor is shown here in 1911 with their three children (left to right), James, Elliot, and Anna.

named Louis Howe to help him. Howe kept Roosevelt's name in the papers so the voters would remember him. On Election Day, Roosevelt won. Louis Howe also became his future advisor.

The following year, Roosevelt helped Woodrow Wilson campaign for the presidency. Like Roosevelt, Wilson was a member of the Democratic Party, one of the two most powerful **political parties** in the nation. When Wilson won, Roosevelt attended his **inauguration,**

13

▸ Franklin Delano Roosevelt is often referred to by his initials, FDR.

▸ The Roosevelts moved to Albany, the New York State capital, after Franklin became a state senator. Away from Franklin's mother, Eleanor was finally able to take charge of her family. "I had to stand on my own two feet," she remembered, "and I think it was good for me. I wanted to be independent."

where he received a wonderful surprise. Wilson wanted him to be the assistant secretary of the U.S. Navy. Roosevelt had always loved ships and sailing. Now he would be a leader of the largest fleet of ships in the world. He would be able to live in the nation's capital and work with the president.

In 1914, Roosevelt ran for the U.S. Senate. He lost the race, however, and returned to his navy job just as World War I was starting in Europe. The United States wanted no part of the war, but Germany sank an American cruise ship, killing 128 people. The German navy did not even try to rescue the survivors. Then in 1917, the Germans announced that they would bomb any ship that entered British waters. President Wilson had no choice at this point. He asked Congress for a **declaration of war.** World War I was a brutal and bloody fight. It finally ended in November of 1918 when the United States and its **allies** won.

Following the war, members of the Democratic Party decided they wanted a change in leadership. In 1920, they held their national convention, a meeting where they chose their presidential **candidate.** They selected James Cox, who asked that Roosevelt run as the vice-presidential candidate. Cox and Roosevelt fought a tough campaign against their opponents, the Republicans. In the end, they lost to Warren G. Harding and his vice president, Calvin Coolidge.

With the Republicans in the White House, Roosevelt had no job. Harding selected Republicans as his assistants. Roosevelt left Washington and tried his hand at business, but he quickly grew bored. He dreamed of a thriving political career—in fact, he dreamed of being president. Roosevelt began planning for the future. "The moment of defeat," he told a friend, "is the best time to plan for victory."

Before he could finish his plans, however, Roosevelt was struck with a staggering challenge. After swimming with his children at Campobello, he became ill. He thought he simply had the flu and went to bed, but his health worsened. His arms and legs ached, and his fever climbed.

Roosevelt had to prepare the navy for World War I. He ordered hundreds of new ships to be built. He also started a recruitment program to enlist thousands of service people. Once the war began, Roosevelt toured naval bases both at home and overseas. During a tour of Europe, he saw firsthand the death and destruction of the war.

▸ After Franklin was struck with polio, Eleanor invited Louis Howe, their friend and advisor, to live at their home for a time. She wanted him to help keep Franklin interested in public affairs and politics.

▸ While working to recover from polio, Franklin Roosevelt often exercised in warm water. In 1924, he visited an old resort in Georgia called Warm Springs. The hot mineral water seemed to help him. He grew to love the resort and invested $200,000 to improve it. He turned it into a treatment center for other polio victims.

The next morning, he collapsed as he tried to get out of bed. By that afternoon, his entire body was **paralyzed.**

The local doctor said Roosevelt merely had a cold. Eleanor and Franklin's advisor, Louis Howe, knew it was much more serious. They talked to a specialist, who said Franklin had polio, a frightening disease that once crippled many children and some adults as well. No one knew how to cure it, and there were few treatments. While Roosevelt worried that his political career might be over, he remained upbeat. He told everyone that he would walk again one day.

Roosevelt worked hard to recover from polio. He exercised daily and especially liked swimming in warm water. Although the paralysis in most of his body disappeared, his legs never fully recovered. He was forced to walk with braces and crutches or to use a wheelchair. For the first time, Roosevelt knew how it felt to be weak. He felt even more sympathy for people who suffered with poverty, illnesses, and handicaps.

Roosevelt returned to politics in 1924 by heading Alfred Smith's campaign for president.

Giving a speech for Smith at the Democratic National Convention took a great deal of courage for Roosevelt. He had always been a strong young man, and now he was crippled. He wanted to stand on his own to give his speech. He brought his son James with him to the convention. James helped his father walk onto the stage, where he stood to speak. The Democrats felt proud to see Roosevelt working to overcome his disability. The crowded room rewarded him with a round of applause.

In 1928, Al Smith asked Roosevelt to run for governor of New York. Roosevelt didn't agree right away. He was still determined to walk again. He didn't want to stop his water therapy. Finally, he agreed for the sake of the Democratic Party. Roosevelt did not think he would win the race, but when the votes were in, he was the new governor of New York.

Roosevelt was reelected in 1930. He served as governor when the **stock market** crashed and the Great Depression began. Before the Depression, many people had invested in the stock market. They had watched their money grow as the market

Interesting Facts

▸ After Roosevelt was paralyzed by polio, he was never able to walk without help again. At first, he thought his career in politics was over. His mother wanted him to retire and live a quiet life at Hyde Park. But Eleanor disagreed. She was certain her husband would recover more quickly if he continued to pursue his interests.

▸ After Roosevelt was elected to a second term as governor, many Democrats wanted him to run for president. Eleanor wasn't sure this was a good idea, but she promised to help him if that was what he wanted to do. "If polio didn't kill him," she once said, "the presidency won't."

climbed to record heights. Then suddenly, the stock market crashed. Thousands of people lost their fortunes. Businesses failed, and people who worked in them lost their jobs. With no income, hungry people lined up at soup kitchens for daily meals. Families lost their homes and were forced to camp in fields using scraps of metal and cardboard boxes as shelters.

By the time Roosevelt was elected governor of New York, he was able to walk again. But he still depended on leg braces, a cane, and a strong arm on which he could lean to help him move.

Roosevelt set up the Temporary Emergency Relief Administration (TERA) to create jobs for the people of his state. TERA workers improved roads, built parks, and cleaned up buildings. News of Roosevelt's successful program spread across the country. People began to talk of him as a future presidential candidate.

NEARLY EVERYONE SUFFERED during the Great Depression. At its worst, 15 million Americans were without jobs. To make ends meet, people did odd jobs, took in ironing, and rented out spare rooms. Many educated and trained workers were forced to sell apples on street corners or shine shoes for change. People begged for jobs. When they couldn't find work, many also begged for money.

"Buddy Can You Spare a Dime?" was a popular song during this time, but no one had a dime. Most Americans couldn't pay their bills, so many store owners took eggs, butter, and cows in trade. Clothes were used and reused. Mothers passed clothes down to younger children and then used what was left for rags or quilt pieces. Women also made clothes or colorful quilts from cotton feed sacks. Most everyone had large gardens, and they canned fruits, vegetables, and meats. Those who had a little money could buy everything cheaply. A nice dress, for example, might have cost $1.

During the Depression, some children quit school because they had no shoes or decent clothes to wear. Others traveled with their families in trucks or wagons from town to town, looking for work and food. Teens from large families often left home. They hitchhiked across the country searching for work and food. Many parents felt ashamed that they couldn't support their families. Because of this, children often played the role of comforters for their parents. During the Great Depression, many children wrote to President and Mrs. Roosevelt, asking them to help their parents.

Chapter THREE

The New Deal

By 1932, it seemed as if Roosevelt's dream of becoming president might come true. The Democratic Party nominated him as its presidential candidate.

DURING THE 1932 CONVENTION, THE Democrats **nominated** Franklin Roosevelt as their presidential candidate. He began campaigning by promising the people a "New Deal." He meant that he wanted to give everyone a second chance. As in a card game, he wanted to deal everyone a new hand.

The people liked what Roosevelt was saying. Many felt that President Herbert Hoover had done little to change the state of the nation during the Depression. The American people needed hope that their lives would improve in the future. On Election Day, Roosevelt enjoyed a sweeping victory, winning in 42 of the 48 states.

Roosevelt's inauguration day in March of 1933 was not the happy celebration that

Outgoing President Hoover rode with Roosevelt to his inauguration on March 4, 1933. Many Americans blamed Hoover for the Great Depression and were eager for a change in leadership. They hoped Roosevelt could do something to help the nation in such troubled times.

other presidents had enjoyed. The country was in desperate trouble. More than a third of American workers did not have jobs. Businesses and banks were shut down. Some people were starving to death.

In his inauguration speech, President Roosevelt told the people, "Let me assert my firm belief that the only thing we have to fear is fear itself." Then Roosevelt laid out goals to open banks, get people back to work, and offer aid to the neediest Americans. His speech was not just talk. For the next three months, known as the "Hundred Days," Roosevelt worked to find solutions. He gathered a wide group of advisors known as the "Brain Trust" to help him. The Brain Trust included people from many professions including professors, lawyers, and **economists.**

One week after his inauguration, Roosevelt announced the Emergency Banking Bill. The bill called for a bank holiday—a period of time when all banks would close. During this time, the weakest banks with little money would simply close their doors for good. Banks with money would reorganize. These stronger banks could reopen quickly but under new laws that would protect their customers' money.

The new banking laws gave people confidence in their banks again. Many people had been hoarding their cash at their homes. Now they felt safe returning it to the bank. Once the banks had more money, they invested it. Money began to circulate through the nation's **economy** again.

President Roosevelt knew that one of the country's biggest problems was the lack of jobs. He and his staff created three programs to help employ workers: the Civil Conservation Corps (CCC), the Civil Works Administration (CWA), and the Works Progress Administration (WPA).

The CCC used government money to hire young men to work outdoors on public projects, such as clearing land and building dams. The CWA hired men and women to work on other government projects, including building libraries and airports. The WPA hired a variety of workers. For instance, it hired writers and artists to create guide-books and public art pieces.

During the Depression, millions of Americans had no jobs. They lined up outside employment agencies, hoping to find work. Roosevelt promised Americans a "New Deal," a fresh start that would improve their lives.

To help those living in the worst conditions, Roosevelt pushed through the Federal Emergency Relief Act (FERA). This set aside $500 million to help the people in the country's neediest cities and counties. Roosevelt also worked to help farmers. Before the Depression, farmers had grown too many crops and could not sell them. Roosevelt set up a system to limit the amount of each crop grown. This way, there would be demand for the crops, and the farmers could sell them for a higher price.

Roosevelt's programs found ways to employ people from many different professions. Artists were employed to teach children how to paint and draw, for example.

The last two measures of the New Deal came only two years after Roosevelt took office. These measures were the Social Security Act of 1935 and the Wagner-Connery Act. The Social Security Act set aside money for those who grew too ill or too old to work. The Wagner-Connery Act allowed workers to band together and form **unions.** With unions, workers could fight as a united force for better wages and working conditions.

Some people felt Roosevelt's programs were dangerous. They did not want Americans to depend so heavily on the government to survive. The wealthy also felt that Roosevelt was going to extreme lengths to help the poor. Yet most Americans agreed with Roosevelt's New Deal.

Although change was slow, the American people gradually began to feel better about their lives. In 1936, they eagerly reelected Franklin Roosevelt as president.

During his second term, both Franklin and Eleanor Roosevelt stayed in touch with the American public. The president regularly had "fireside chats" over the radio to explain what was occurring in the country. Families gathered around the radio to listen to their great leader's calming voice. Mrs. Roosevelt toured the country and was the president's eyes and ears. She listened to the people's problems and thought of ways to help them. She reported back to the president about what she saw and heard.

As President Roosevelt worked to heal the economy, he saw a serious situation brewing in other parts of the world. Germany, Italy, and Japan seemed determined to take over the world by force. America could stay at a safe distance for a while, but the country's European allies could not. In fact, it wasn't long before nearly all of Europe was involved in World War II. Americans watched the war unfold with horror and fear.

WHEN FRANKLIN ROOSEVELT BECAME ASSISTANT SECRETARY OF THE NAVY, the Roosevelts moved to Washington, D.C. FDR loved their busy life in Washington, but Eleanor did not. A politician's wife was expected to be friendly and entertaining. Yet Eleanor felt awkward at the parties and social events. Often she would stay home.

In 1918, something happened that made Eleanor feel even more insecure. After 13 years of marriage, Eleanor discovered that her husband was having a love affair with her secretary, Lucy Mercer. Of course Eleanor was devastated. "All my self-confidence is gone and I am on the edge," she wrote in her journal. Although Franklin worked hard to fix their marriage, it was never quite the same.

Oddly, Franklin Roosevelt's love affair and his successful career began to push Eleanor to become independent. Roosevelt's advisor, Louis Howe, also helped Eleanor gain confidence. He encouraged her to make speeches and travel across the country because Franklin could not.

When she became first lady, Eleanor decided it was time to come into her own. She took up serious causes and charities and made friends with other educated women. Eleanor joined the League of Women Voters and became a leader in the women's division of the Democratic Party. As first lady, Mrs. Roosevelt was called "Eleanor Everywhere" because she traveled constantly to visit with the American people. Mrs. Roosevelt also wrote columns, gave lectures, and was interviewed on the radio. She was the author of many books on a variety of subjects.

Eleanor Roosevelt's greatest work was the Universal Declaration of Human Rights. In 1946, following President Roosevelt's death, she was elected chairperson of the United Nations Human Rights Commission. The job of the commission was to ensure basic rights for all people around the world. These rights included the right to an education and to free speech. After two years of hard work, the United Nations passed the Universal Declaration of Human Rights that described these basic rights.

Eleanor Roosevelt died in 1962 at age 78. She was buried next to President Roosevelt in the rose garden at the Hyde Park mansion.

Chapter FOUR

Fight for a Free World

As Roosevelt prepared for the election of 1940, problems in Europe were growing serious. He feared that the United States might again be forced to go to war.

DURING WORLD WAR II, ADOLF HITLER ruled Germany. Hitler came to power when Germany was struggling with even bigger problems than the United States. All of Europe was suffering from the Depression. Germany also had to pay back huge debts after losing World War I. The German people wanted solutions to their problems. Hitler was a smart but evil man who was also an excellent speaker. He blamed all Germany's problems on other countries and on the Jewish people of his own country, many of whom were bankers.

In 1940, Germany invaded Norway, Denmark, and Belgium. Then Hitler advanced on Holland and finally France. Winston Churchill was the Prime Minister

Adolf Hitler led the Nazi political party in Germany, which was in power from 1933 through 1945. The Nazis believed in protecting the German culture. They blamed the Jewish people and other nations for all their problems. By the end of World War II, the Nazis had brutally murdered people who they believed were enemies of the German people.

of Great Britain at the time. He begged President Roosevelt to send navy ships to help fight the Germans. Roosevelt did not want to get involved in the war, but he knew he had to help. In the end, he lent England 50 ships.

▶ As Germany and Italy aggressively attacked Europe and Japan waged war in Asia, Roosevelt knew the United States would soon be forced to help. "We must try to prevent the domination of the world," he said, "but I am not willing to fire the first shot. I am waiting to be pushed into the situation."

▶ The Republican who ran against Roosevelt in the election of 1940, Wendell Willkie, was once a Democrat. In fact, he contributed $150 to Roosevelt's first campaign for president. Over the years, he disagreed with Roosevelt on certain policies and became a Republican.

Fearing that Americans would soon have to fight, Roosevelt passed the Selective Service Act (SSA) before the next presidential election. The SSA required every man aged 21 or older to register to serve in the military if needed. This was a risky move for an election year, but Roosevelt felt the country should be prepared.

During the 1940 campaign for president, the Republican candidate, Wendell Willkie, criticized Roosevelt for helping England. He and others voiced fears that Roosevelt was moving America into the war. After World War I and the Great Depression, most Americans did not want to face such a frightening ordeal. Even with such criticism, Roosevelt was easily elected to a third term as president.

As the American people learned more about the war, they began to feel outraged at Germany and its allies. They saw films and photos of the Germans bombing England, a country closely tied to the United States. They listened to Winston Churchill make moving speeches on the radio about the horrors of the German Nazis. They also heard stories of Japan invading other Asian countries.

Gradually, Americans realized that they might have to enter the war to stop these horrors from spreading to American shores.

The Japanese finally made it clear that the United States would have to fight. On December 7, 1941, the Japanese bombed Pearl Harbor in Hawaii. This act killed 2,403 Americans and wounded nearly 1,200. The next day, the United States declared war. "No matter how long it may take us," President Roosevelt stated in a radio address, "the American people in their righteous might will win through to absolute victory."

After the Japanese bombed Pearl Harbor on December 7, 1941, Americans felt they had no choice but to enter the war.

The war changed the United States practically overnight. Young men began to sign up for the military and train for battle. Women stepped in and took the jobs that the men left. The economy quickly recovered as factories geared up to supply the armed forces. Everyone united and became part of the war effort.

The war was a difficult time for President Roosevelt. Just before Pearl Harbor, his mother died. In addition, he was concerned for his four sons, who had enlisted in the armed forces. Still the Roosevelts remained strong for the American people. In his fireside chats, President Roosevelt assured the people that the government was doing everything possible to win the war. Mrs. Roosevelt helped the Red Cross and knitted sweaters and socks for U.S. troops. She even traveled overseas to visit wounded soldiers.

The poster below shows an injured soldier from Pearl Harbor. It asked Americans to buy bonds, which were investments that would help support the war effort.

During World War II, England, Russia, and the United States were known as the Allies. The main goal of the Allies was to take back the countries of Europe. They planned "Operation Torch," led by U.S. General Dwight D. Eisenhower and British General Sir Bernard Montgomery. Through Operation Torch, the Allies freed North Africa and were able to make their way into Europe.

Once they had a foothold in Europe, the Allies prepared for the invasion that would be the turning point in the war. Roosevelt and Churchill carefully planned this invasion, code-named "D-Day," on the French shore

Interesting Facts

▸ After Japan bombed Pearl Harbor, many people feared that Japanese Americans might be more loyal to Japan than to the United States. In 1942, Roosevelt issued an order that allowed the military to confine people of Japanese descent. More than 110,000 Japanese people—two-thirds of whom were born in the United States— were moved to guarded camps. Most stayed in these camps until the end of the war.

During World War II, women took over the jobs that men had left behind when they went to war. Americans united and worked to help the nation march toward victory.

of Normandy. On D-Day, the Allies staged a giant invasion from the water. Losses were great on both sides, but the Allies won the battle and were able to drive the Germans out of France over the next few months.

Americans also won huge victories against the Japanese in the South Pacific. Yet the war raged on. By the next election in 1944, Roosevelt was exhausted. He accepted his party's nomination, but he did not feel it was right to campaign. "In these days of tragic sorrow, I do not consider it fitting," he said. Harry Truman was chosen as the vice presidential candidate.

Roosevelt won a fourth term as president and continued his work to win World War II. Roosevelt met with Churchill and Joseph Stalin, the leader of Russia, at the Yalta Conference. Although neither Roosevelt nor Churchill trusted Stalin, they needed him to win the war. The "Big Three," as they were called, felt certain that an Allied victory was right around the corner. They made plans for the end of the war. Roosevelt returned from his meeting very tired. For the first time, he addressed Congress in his wheelchair instead of standing with his crutches.

In February of 1945, Roosevelt met with Winston Churchill (seated, right) and Joseph Stalin (seated, left) at the Yalta Conference. The three leaders met to discuss what would happen at the end of the war. One important agreement at the event was to establish the United Nations. This important organization is a union of countries that work for peace and for the welfare of people around the world.

Left: Roosevelt made sure that photographs were rarely taken of him in his wheelchair. He felt Americans would have more confidence in him if they did not think of him as crippled. He is shown here in 1941 with his dog Fala and the granddaughter of a family friend.

Right: After President Roosevelt returned to the United States, he reported the events of the Yalta Conference. He spoke unevenly and looked thin and tired. Many Americans worried that he was not well. A month and a half later, he died, leaving the nation to wonder what would happen without his trusted leadership.

Interesting Facts

▶ The Germans surrendered on May 7, 1945, ending the war in Europe. The war raged on in Asia for several more months before the Japanese surrendered on August 14, 1945.

Franklin Delano Roosevelt did not live to see the final victory of the Allies in World War II. On April 12, 1945, he died in Warm Springs, Georgia, of a massive brain **hemorrhage.** It was just 25 days before the Germans **surrendered** and the war in Europe was over. Roosevelt's death deeply saddened Americans, who had counted on his steady guidance through more than 12 years of trying times. Just before his death, Roosevelt had been writing a speech for Thomas Jefferson Day. "The only limits to our realization of tomorrow will be our doubts of today," he wrote in his reassuring manner. "Let us move forward with strong, active faith."

IN AUGUST OF 1939, the famous scientist Albert Einstein sent a letter to President Roosevelt about a new type of nuclear power. This power could be used to make a deadly weapon called the atomic bomb. He warned the president of the horrible danger that might occur if Germany or another hostile nation built an atomic bomb first. Roosevelt listened.

In 1942, the U.S. government began the top-secret Manhattan Project to develop an atomic bomb. In 1945, at a test site in New Mexico, the government tested the first atomic bomb. During the entire war, both the United States and Great Britain believed that German scientists were working on a similar weapon.

After Roosevelt's death, Vice President Truman became president. The war in Europe ended quickly after Hitler committed suicide and Germany surrendered. But the war in Asia continued, with great loss of American lives.

President Truman made a difficult decision. He decided to use atomic weapons to end the war. He warned the Japanese that if they did not surrender, their nation would suffer complete destruction. But the Japanese would not give up.

In August of 1945, the United States dropped two atomic bombs on the Japanese cities of Hiroshima and Nagasaki within a few days of each other. More than 100,000 people were killed, and even more were terribly injured from severe burns. Japan finally surrendered eight days after the first bomb was dropped.

1882 On January 30, Franklin Delano Roosevelt (FDR) is born in Hyde Park, New York, to James and Sara Roosevelt.

1896 FDR enters Groton boarding school in Massachusetts at age 14.

1900 FDR enters Harvard College in Cambridge, Massachusetts.

1903 On June 24, FDR graduates from Harvard.

1904 FDR enters Columbia Law School. His cousin, Theodore Roosevelt, wins the presidential election in November.

1905 On March 17, Franklin Roosevelt marries Anna Eleanor Roosevelt.

1907 FDR passes the New York State law exam and is able to work as a lawyer. He begins work as a law clerk at the law firm of Carter, Ledyard, and Milburn in New York City.

1910 FDR is elected to the New York State Senate.

1913 President Wilson appoints FDR assistant secretary of the U.S. Navy.

1914 FDR is defeated in an election for the U.S. Senate. World War I begins.

1917 The United States enters World War I.

1918 World War I ends on November 11.

1920 FDR is nominated for vice president at the Democratic National Convention. James Cox is the presidential candidate. Republicans Warren G. Harding and Calvin Coolidge defeat Cox and Roosevelt.

1921 Roosevelt contracts polio after swimming at Campobello in August.

1924 FDR reenters politics as manager of Alfred E. Smith's presidential campaign. Smith loses the race.

1927 FDR founds the Georgia Warm Springs Foundation, a therapy center for the treatment of polio victims.

1928 FDR is elected governor of New York.

1929 The stock market crashes, and the Great Depression begins.

1930 FDR is reelected governor. The Bank of the United States and its many branches close.

1932 FDR is elected president.

1933 FDR survives an assassination attempt in Florida. On March 4, he is inaugurated as the 32nd president. During the first 100 days of his presidency, Roosevelt presents a wide variety of projects to help end the Depression. His plans are known as the "New Deal."

1935 FDR signs the U.S. Social Security Act and the Wagner-Connery Act, the latter of which allows workers to form labor unions.

1936 FDR is reelected president. He wins the election in every state but two, Maine and Vermont.

1940 As Germany invades other European nations, FDR sends ships to help Great Britain fight the Germans. Knowing the United States may have to enter the war, FDR passes the Selective Service Act, which requires men aged 21 and older to sign up for military service if needed. In November, FDR wins a third presidential election.

1941 On December 7, Japan bombs Pearl Harbor. The United States declares war on Japan. On December 11, Germany and Italy declare war on the United States. As commander-in-chief of the armed forces, FDR helps plan major offensives in the war.

1942 The U.S. government transfers more than 110,000 Japanese Americans to camps.

1944 D-Day occurs on June 6. By the end of the summer, the Allies successfully drive Germany out of France. FDR is reelected president on November 7. He is the only American president to be elected four times.

1945 In February, FDR attends the Yalta Convention with Winston Churchill and Joseph Stalin. The three leaders discuss what will happen at the end of the war and establish the United Nations. On April 12, Franklin Roosevelt dies in Warm Springs, Georgia. He is buried in Hyde Park, New York. Harry Truman takes over the duties of the president. Germany surrenders 25 days after FDR's death, ending the war in Europe. The United States drops atomic bombs on Japan in August. Japan surrenders, and World War II ends.

1962 On November 7, Eleanor Roosevelt dies after suffering a severe stroke.

allies (AL-lize)
Allies are nations that have agreed to help each other by fighting together against a common enemy. In World War II, Russia and England were allies of the United States.

amendment (uh-MEND-ment)
An amendment is a change or addition made to the U.S. Constitution or other documents. The 22nd Amendment states that no president can hold office for more than two terms.

campaign (kam-PAYN)
If people campaign, they take part in activities to win an election, including giving speeches or attending rallies. Roosevelt campaigned across New York to become a state senator.

candidate (KAN-dih-det)
A candidate is a person running in an election. The Democrats chose Roosevelt as their vice presidential candidate in 1920.

constitution (kon-stih-TOO-shun)
A constitution is the set of basic principles that govern a state, country, or society. The 22nd Amendment to the U.S. Constitution was approved in 1951.

declaration of war (dek-luh-RAY-shun OF WAR)
In the United States, a declaration of war is a formal statement that the country is entering a conflict with another country. A declaration of war is usually given by the president and then approved by Congress.

depression (dih-PRESH-un)
A depression is a period of time in which there is little business activity, and many people are out of work. The Great Depression began in 1929.

economists (ee-KON-uh-mists)
Economists are people who study the economy. Roosevelt asked economists to help him find ways to end the Depression.

economy (ee-KON-uh-mee)
The economy is the way money is earned and spent in a country or area. The United States economy collapsed after the stock market crash of 1929.

hemorrhage (HEM-er-rij)
A hemorrhage is uncontrollable bleeding in part of the body. Roosevelt died of a severe brain hemorrhage in 1945.

**inauguration
(ih-nawg-yuh-RAY-shun)**
An inauguration is the ceremony that takes place when a new president begins a term. Roosevelt attended President Wilson's inauguration.

nominate (NOM-ih-nayt)
If a political party nominates someone, it chooses him or her to run for a political office. In 1932, the Democrats nominated Franklin Roosevelt as their presidential candidate.

paralyzed (PAIR-eh-lyzd)
If someone is paralyzed, he or she cannot move parts of the body. Roosevelt was paralyzed by polio.

**political parties
(puh-LIT-ih-kul PAR-teez)**
A political party is a group of people who share similar ideas about how to run a government. Roosevelt belonged to the Democratic political party.

politics (PAWL-ih-tiks)
Politics refers to the actions and practices of the government. Roosevelt had a strong interest in politics as a young boy.

stock market (STOK MAR-kit)
The stock market is where people buy and sell pieces of ownership in different companies, called "shares" or "stock." After the stock market crash of 1929, millions of Americans lost their businesses and jobs.

surrender (suh-REN-dur)
If an army surrenders, it gives up to its enemy. Germany surrendered just 25 days after Roosevelt's death.

term (TERM)
A term is the length of time a politician can keep his or her position by law. A U.S. president's term is four years.

unions (YOON-yenz)
Unions are groups of people, such as workers, who join together to accomplish a goal. The Wagner-Connery Act allowed workers to form unions.

Our PRESIDENTS

President	Birthplace	Life Span	Presidency	Political Party	First Lady
George Washington	Virginia	1732–1799	1789–1797	None	Martha Dandridge Custis Washington
John Adams	Massachusetts	1735–1826	1797–1801	Federalist	Abigail Smith Adams
Thomas Jefferson	Virginia	1743–1826	1801–1809	Democratic-Republican	widower
James Madison	Virginia	1751–1836	1809–1817	Democratic Republican	Dolley Payne Todd Madison
James Monroe	Virginia	1758–1831	1817–1825	Democratic Republican	Elizabeth Kortright Monroe
John Quincy Adams	Massachusetts	1767–1848	1825–1829	Democratic-Republican	Louisa Johnson Adams
Andrew Jackson	South Carolina	1767–1845	1829–1837	Democrat	widower
Martin Van Buren	New York	1782–1862	1837–1841	Democrat	widower
William H. Harrison	Virginia	1773–1841	1841	Whig	Anna Symmes Harrison
John Tyler	Virginia	1790–1862	1841–1845	Whig	Letitia Christian Tyler / Julia Gardiner Tyler
James K. Polk	North Carolina	1795–1849	1845–1849	Democrat	Sarah Childress Polk

Our PRESIDENTS

President	Birthplace	Life Span	Presidency	Political Party	First Lady
Zachary Taylor	Virginia	1784–1850	1849–1850	Whig	Margaret Mackall Smith Taylor
Millard Fillmore	New York	1800–1874	1850–1853	Whig	Abigail Powers Fillmore
Franklin Pierce	New Hampshire	1804–1869	1853–1857	Democrat	Jane Means Appleton Pierce
James Buchanan	Pennsylvania	1791–1868	1857–1861	Democrat	never married
Abraham Lincoln	Kentucky	1809–1865	1861–1865	Republican	Mary Todd Lincoln
Andrew Johnson	North Carolina	1808–1875	1865–1869	Democrat	Eliza McCardle Johnson
Ulysses S. Grant	Ohio	1822–1885	1869–1877	Republican	Julia Dent Grant
Rutherford B. Hayes	Ohio	1822–1893	1877–1881	Republican	Lucy Webb Hayes
James A. Garfield	Ohio	1831–1881	1881	Republican	Lucretia Rudolph Garfield
Chester A. Arthur	Vermont	1829–1886	1881–1885	Republican	widower
Grover Cleveland	New Jersey	1837–1908	1885–1889	Democrat	Frances Folsom Cleveland

Our PRESENTS

President	Birthplace	Life Span	Presidency	Political Party	First Lady
Benjamin Harrison	Ohio	1833–1901	1889–1893	Republican	Caroline Scott Harrison
Grover Cleveland	New Jersey	1837–1908	1893–1897	Democrat	Frances Folsom Cleveland
William McKinley	Ohio	1843–1901	1897–1901	Republican	Ida Saxton McKinley
Theodore Roosevelt	New York	1858–1919	1901–1909	Republican	Edith Kermit Carow Roosevelt
William H. Taft	Ohio	1857–1930	1909–1913	Republican	Helen Herron Taft
Woodrow Wilson	Virginia	1856–1924	1913–1921	Democrat	Ellen L. Axson Wilson Edith Bolling Galt Wilson
Warren G. Harding	Ohio	1865–1923	1921–1923	Republican	Florence Kling De Wolfe Harding
Calvin Coolidge	Vermont	1872–1933	1923–1929	Republican	Grace Goodhue Coolidge
Herbert C. Hoover	Iowa	1874–1964	1929–1933	Republican	Lou Henry Hoover
Franklin D. Roosevelt	New York	1882–1945	1933–1945	Democrat	Anna Eleanor Roosevelt Roosevelt
Harry S. Truman	Missouri	1884–1972	1945–1953	Democrat	Elizabeth Wallace Truman

Our PRESIDENTS

President	Birthplace	Life Span	Presidency	Political Party	First Lady
Dwight D. Eisenhower	Texas	1890–1969	1953–1961	Republican	Mary "Mamie" Doud Eisenhower
John F. Kennedy	Massachusetts	1917–1963	1961–1963	Democrat	Jacqueline Bouvier Kennedy
Lyndon B. Johnson	Texas	1908–1973	1963–1969	Democrat	Claudia Alta Taylor Johnson
Richard M. Nixon	California	1913–1994	1969–1974	Republican	Thelma Catherine Ryan Nixon
Gerald Ford	Nebraska	1913–	1974–1977	Republican	Elizabeth "Betty" Bloomer Warren Ford
James Carter	Georgia	1924–	1977–1981	Democrat	Rosalynn Smith Carter
Ronald Reagan	Illinois	1911–	1981–1989	Republican	Nancy Davis Reagan
George Bush	Massachusetts	1924–	1989–1993	Republican	Barbara Pierce Bush
William Clinton	Arkansas	1946–	1993–2001	Democrat	Hillary Rodham Clinton
George W. Bush	Connecticut	1946–	2001–	Republican	Laura Welch Bush

Presidential Facts

Qualifications
To run for president, a candidate must
- be at least 35 years old
- be a citizen who was born in the United States
- have lived in the United States for 14 years

Term of Office
A president's term of office is four years. No president can stay in office for more than two terms.

Election Date
The presidential election takes place every four years on the first Tuesday of November.

Inauguration Date
Presidents are inaugurated on January 20.

Oath of Office
I do solemnly swear I will faithfully execute the office of the President of the United States and will to the best of my ability preserve, protect, and defend the Constitution of the United States.

Write a Letter to the President
One of the best things about being a U.S. citizen is that Americans get to participate in their government. They can speak out if they feel government leaders aren't doing their jobs. They can also praise leaders who are going the extra mile. Do you have something you'd like the president to do? Should the president worry more about the environment and encourage people to recycle? Should the government spend more money on our schools? You can write a letter to the president to say how you feel!

1600 Pennsylvania Avenue
Washington, D.C. 20500

You can even send an e-mail to: president@whitehouse.gov

For Further INFORMATION

Internet Sites

Visit the Franklin D. Roosevelt Library, located in Hyde Park, New York:
http://www.fdrlibrary.marist.edu/

Explore the life and accomplishments of President Roosevelt:
http://www.usdreams.com/RooseveltF24.html

Learn more about Eleanor Roosevelt:
http://www.udhr50.org/history/Biographies/bioer.htm

Learn more about FDR and the New Deal:
http://www.geocities.com/Athens/4545/

Read transcripts of Roosevelt's fireside chats:
http://www.mhrcc.org/fdr/fdr.html

View thousands of photos from the Great Depression and World War II:
http://memory.loc.gov/ammem/fsowhome.html

Learn more about World War I:
http://www.pbs.org/greatwar/

Learn more about Word War II:
http://nav.webring.org/cgi-bin/navcgi?ring=ww2;list

Books

Freedman, Russel. *Eleanor Roosevelt, A Life of Discovery.* New York: Clarion Books, 1993.

Gay, Kathlyn and Martin. *World War II.* New York: Twenty-First Century Books, 1995.

Kehret, Peg. *Small Steps: The Year I Got Polio.* Morton Grove, IL: Albert Whitman & Co., 1996.

Kent, Zachary. *World War I, "The War to End Wars."* Springfield, NJ: Enslow Publishers, 1994.

Millichap, Nancy. *The Stock Market Crash of 1929.* New York: New Discovery Books, 1994.

Ross, Stewart. *Causes and Consequences of the Great Depression.* Austin, TX: Steck-Vaughn Raintree, 1998.

Schuman, Michael A. *Franklin D. Roosevelt, The Four-Term President.* Springfield, NJ: Enslow Publishers, 1996.

Index